123 Healthy Me

Written by
Priya Patel

Illustrated by
Puja Suri

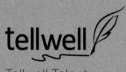

Tellwell Talent
www.tellwell.ca

ISBN
978-0-2288-5179-0 (Hardcover)
978-0-2288-5178-3 (Paperback)

1 2 3 Healthy Me

Let's go to the market and see what's fresh.

What's in these bags? Can you guess?

What ingredients shall we use?
Let's take a look!

1

head of
**white
cauliflower,**
seasoned and
ready to roast.

A dinner with friends we are ready to host.

We add spice and sautée. Cooking is a blast!

3 purple
eggplants,
ready to slice.

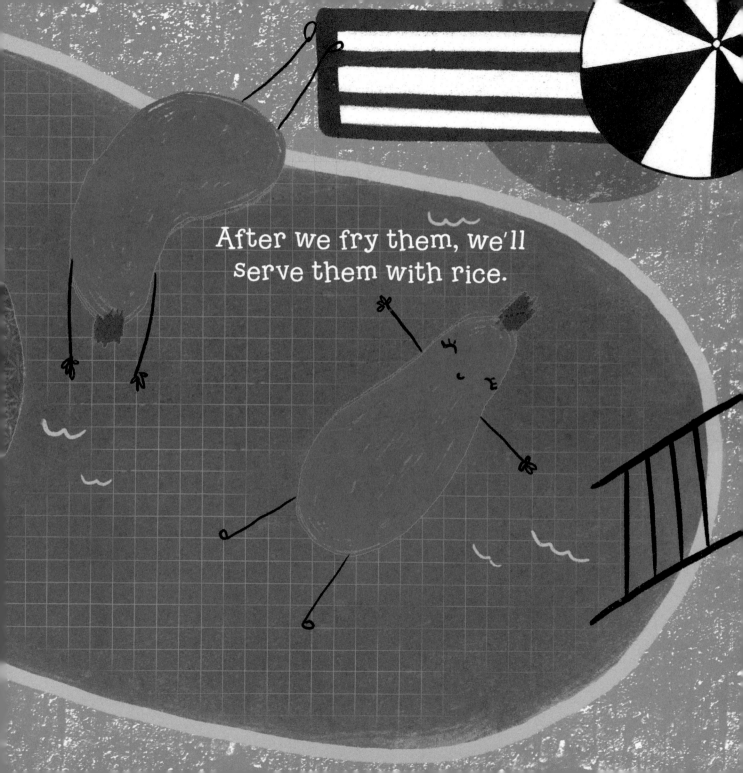

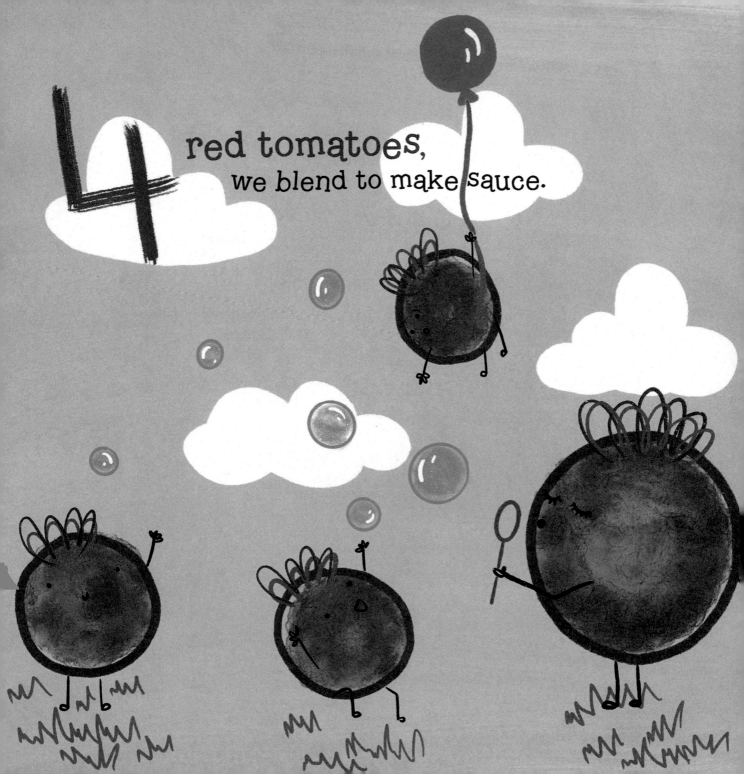

We'll mix it with veggies
and give them a toss.

5 orange sweet potatoes,
we cut and then broil.

Into the oven they go,
with a dash of sea salt and oil.

6 green zucchinis, we carefully grate.

Delicious and tasty mixed with
veggies on our plate.

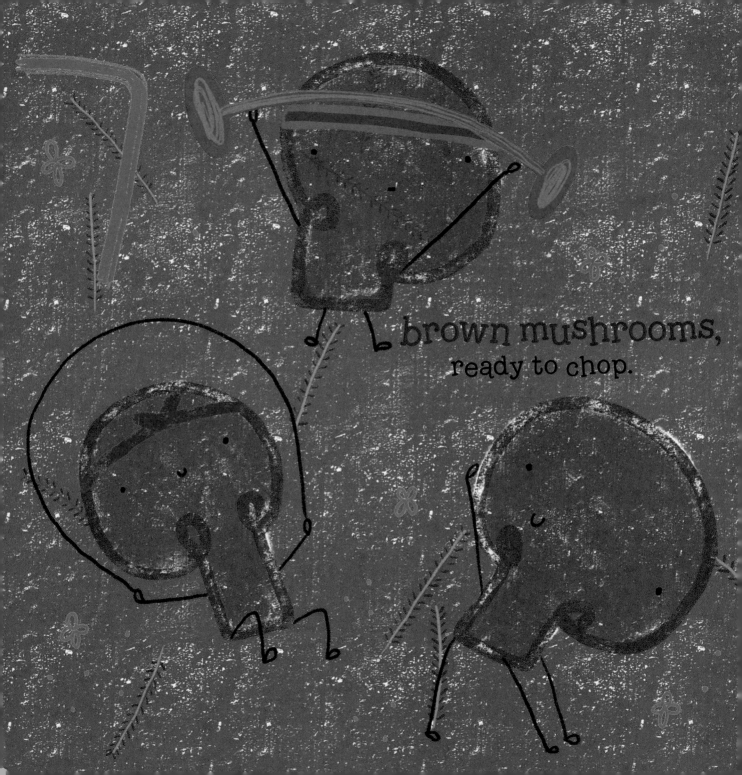

brown mushrooms,
ready to chop.

How yummy they will be,
with sauce on top.

8 pieces of
green broccoli,
delicious when steamed.

spoons of **black beans,**
we boil and stew.

It's almost time to eat.
I'm hungry. Are you?

10 friends for dinner. Let's be thankful for our meal.

Happy and healthy is how we will feel!

Made in the USA
Monee, IL
14 July 2021